# Halley's
# Comet

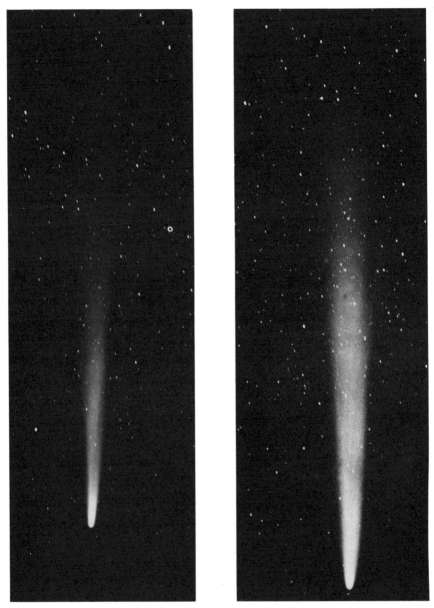

*Halley's Comet photographed from Honolulu on May 12 and 15, 1910.*

# Halley's Comet

Norman D. Anderson
and
Walter R. Brown

*Illustrated with photographs and prints*

**Dodd, Mead & Company**
New York

ILLUSTRATION CREDITS

Ambroise Pare's *Livres de Chirurgie*, Paris, 1597, 11; Emerson's *Comet Lore*, 1910, 38, 47; Lick Observatory, 20; Mallet's Description de L'Universe, Paris, 1683, 15; *Mexico Herald*, 34; Mount Wilson and Las Campanas Observatories, Carnegie Institution of Washington, 2, 44; NASA, 51, 54; *Outlook*, vol. 93, 1909, 8, 41; Annual Report of Smithsonian Institution, 1909, 9; Yerkes Observatory Photograph, 12, 17, 25, 31, 32, 37, 39, 42, 45, 46, 62, 70; drawings by Steve Daniels, 18, 30, 43, 50, 56, 58; photographs by Todd Anderson, 24, 26, 66, 67, 68.

1   2   3   4   5   6   7   8   9   10

Library of Congress Cataloging in Publication Data

Anderson, Norman D.
Halley's comet.

Includes index.
Summary: Describes the discovery of Halley's comet
and its historic significance. Also briefly discusses
what is known of the composition of comets and their
relationship to the earth.
1. Halley's comet—Juvenile literature.   [1. Halley's
comet.   2. Comets]   I. Brown, Walter R., 1929-
II. Title.
QB723.H2A56          523.6′4          81-3314
ISBN 0-396-07974-1                     AACR2

# Contents

# 1.

# Comets
# in Ancient Times

From the very earliest times, people watched the skies and wondered about what they saw. They noted how lights and objects in the sky changed and moved, from day to day and month to month. They realized that these changes took place in regular patterns. The sun rose in the east every morning, traveled across the sky, and set in the west. The shape of the moon changed a little each night, and about every 29 days it started its pattern of change all over again. Even the stars and the planets changed their positions in the sky over a year's time.

Because the changes in the skies followed regular patterns, ancient people learned to predict the changes. They knew the times of sunrise and sunset, and when there would be a full moon. Although they did not understand what caused these changes, they knew what to expect and when. Because of this, they were not afraid of many of the things they saw in the sky.

But there were some changes they could not predict. Sometimes a star seemed to fall from its place in the sky. At other

*People in ancient times were terrified of comets. This is a drawing of a comet in the Middle Ages.*

times a terrifying ball of fire flashed through the air. Once in a while the sun slowly disappeared and then reappeared in the middle of the day. Or the moon would do the same thing—slowly disappear and then appear again within a few hours' time. These kinds of changes could not be predicted at all. No one knew when they would happen, and so people were frightened of them. And they made up fantastic stories to explain what they saw. When the sun disappeared in an eclipse, the Chinese imagined that dragons were eating the sun. Banging on gongs and drums was supposed to scare the dragons away.

The change in the sky that frightened people the most was the comet. It would seem to start as a new star. Then, night after night, it would grow larger and brighter. After several weeks, a huge tail would start to grow from the star. Sometimes this tail would stretch across the night sky from horizon to horizon. To the frightened people it looked like a giant flaming sword hanging

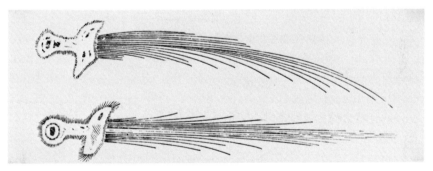

*Comets were thought to look like "flaming swords" in the sky.*

above them. Sometimes it stayed in the sky for a month or more.

Such a strange sight had to be a warning of some kind, they thought. The "flaming swords" must mean that some kind of disaster would occur—a famine, a flood, war, or the death of a mighty king. Of course, these things often happened anyway, whether there was a comet in the sky or not. But when comets were seen, they were often given the blame for any disaster that followed.

Ancient records from Arabia report that a comet in the year 1732 B.C. caused a terrible famine. The Roman leader, Julius Caesar, was killed at a time when there was supposed to have been a comet in the sky. Another Roman Emperor, Nero, also died with a comet in the heavens.

Some people have killed themselves because they thought that comets foretold their deaths. Hannibal was one of the greatest military leaders the world has ever seen. In 184 B.C. a comet seemed to hang over him for three months. Hannibal's fortune-teller said that it was a sign that the leader was going to die. The prediction frightened the great general so much that he killed himself by taking poison.

A French doctor described the great comet that seemed to hang over Paris in 1528. He said it was dark red, almost the color of blood, and was shaped like a bent arm. The hand of the arm held a great sword, ready to strike the helpless city. There were axes, knives, and smaller swords surrounding the larger sword. Several horrible faces appeared near the comet, each with huge beards and long, bristling hair. The doctor reported that many people died of fear and that many others became ill.

Scientists now know that comets usually have very little effect on the earth. But comets can be spectacular sights. It is no wonder that people were alarmed by the strange, brilliant light that appeared in the sky. They had no idea what a comet was or what caused it.

Astronomers—scientists who study the universe outside the earth's atmosphere—are not certain what comets are made of. They think that comets are nothing but tiny bits of dust and a lot

*A drawing of the fearful comet of 1528, as described by a French doctor.*

of frozen gas. One astronomer has called a comet "a bag full of nothing."

Comets come in different sizes. The Great Comet of 1811 had a head that was bigger than the sun, and a comet in 1843 had a tail 200 million miles long. But some comets have no tails at all and look like merely fuzzy patches in the sky. "Hairy stars"—as

11

*Halley's Comet, with its long tail, on May 29, 1910*

some people have called them—would be a good name for them.

Comets do not shine by themselves. The light of the sun makes the comet glow as it nears the sun. The nearer the comet gets to the sun, the brighter it becomes. Once it goes around the sun and heads back toward outer space, it quickly fades.

Scientists now know that the appearance of many comets can be predicted. Most comets follow a pattern that is almost as regular as the patterns of the sun and moon. Astronomers can predict almost exactly when a particular comet will be in the sky. They can do this, even though they can see the comet for only a few weeks or months each time it passes near the earth.

This ability to know and understand the travels of comets through space is due largely to the work of one man. His name was Edmund Halley. This scientist did not discover the comet named after him, but his studies of it made it famous.

# 2.

# Who Was
# Edmund Halley?

Edmund Halley was born in London, England, in 1656. His father was a wealthy man and was able to send Edmund to college at Oxford. While he was there, the young man studied both mathematics and astronomy. By the time he was twenty, he had written his first scientific study of the movements of the planets.

Edmund's father gave him enough money so that he could travel in the Southern Hemisphere for two years. During this time, Halley made a catalog of the southern stars. To do this, he learned how to build and use a telescope. His catalog of southern stars made him one of the most famous astronomers in Europe. At the time, he was still a young man, only twenty-two years old.

Like most astronomers of his time, Halley was interested in comets. A huge, bright comet appeared in the sky during the year 1682. Halley studied it carefully. He took many measurements of the comet's path as it traveled slowly across the sky. But then the young scientist became interested in other things. He put his figures aside.

*A drawing made in the seventeenth century showing different types of comets.*

During the next twenty years, Edmund Halley did many things. He went to sea several times to try to find ways to measure the exact position of ships. He also studied why the ship's compass did not always point due north. For a while, he was in charge of the Royal Mint of England, where he supervised the making of coins. And he worked for a time as an engineer in the building of a fort at Trieste, a city that is now a part of Italy.

It was not until 1704 that Edmund Halley found time to return to his study of comets. In that year he was hired as a teacher of mathematics at Oxford University. This job gave him the time he needed for his observations of comets.

Most scientists of that day thought that comets were bodies that came from deep space far beyond the solar system. They felt sure that comets wandered through space until they happened to come close to the sun. The gravity of the sun attracted the comet, they thought, and pulled it in. They believed that many comets were pulled into the sun and destroyed. If the comet missed being pulled into the sun, they thought that it swung around the sun and returned to space. It was very unlikely, they were sure, that a comet would ever return to the solar system a second time.

Halley could, of course, only see a comet during a small part of its travels through space. This was that part of the comet's path, or orbit, closest to the sun. To see how this was a problem, imagine for a moment that you are standing near a tree in the woods. You represent the earth and the nearby tree is the sun. Suddenly a runner comes out of the woods and heads toward you. As he draws close, he runs around you and the tree and then disappears back into the woods near the point where you first saw him. You can describe his path while you have him in sight, but can you describe his path when he is in the woods out of your sight?

*Edmund Halley, who correctly predicted the return of the comet that bears his name.*

In spite of Halley being able to see only part of a comet's orbit, it was enough for him to figure out the kind of curved path in which it traveled. His figures showed him that many comets did not swing around the sun and fly off into space, as many scientists believed. Halley checked and rechecked his mathematics. To his surprise, his figures seemed correct. They showed that at least some comets followed an orbit called an "ellipse."

An ellipse is a path something like a squashed circle. The orbits followed by the earth and other planets around the sun are ellipses. If comets followed elliptical paths, they would not fly off into space and be lost. Instead, they would return to orbit the sun again and again.

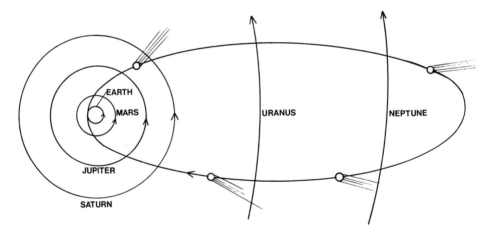

*The orbit of Halley's Comet*

Halley's figures showed that the comet he had seen in 1682 followed an elliptical path. He went over his measurements of this comet again. Remember that this was at a time before computers, calculators, or even adding machines. All mathematical problems had to be solved with pen and paper. It took Halley days and even weeks to solve a single problem. But he had to be certain that he was right. Every time, he came up with the same answer. The 1682 comet followed an elliptical path that took it nearly $3\frac{1}{2}$ billion miles away from the sun and then back again.

Excitedly, Halley looked through the records scientists had made of comets that had been seen in the past. He found two that followed almost exactly the same path as the one he had studied. These had passed the sun in 1607 and in 1531. Could it be that all three comets were really the same one?

There was one problem, however, with his idea. The time between the passing of the comet in 1531 and in 1607 was 76 years. But the time between 1607 and 1682 was only 75 years. Why, if this was the same comet, were the times between trips different?

Halley's first scientific research, done when he was only twenty years old, had been on the motion of the planets. He knew that the elliptical paths of Jupiter and Saturn were not always what he expected them to be. He guessed that this difference was caused by the pull of gravity of the two huge bodies on each other. The gravity of the sun kept them in their elliptical orbits. But, when they passed each other, they were both pulled slightly off their predicted paths.

Halley thought that perhaps this was what was happening to the comet he was studying. As it swung close to the huge planets, their gravitational pull would slow the comet down enough to make it arrive a year behind schedule. If, on the other hand, Jupiter and Saturn were not close to the path of the comet, the speed of the comet would not be changed.

Halley went to work with pen and paper again. This time he tried to figure where Saturn and Jupiter would be on the comet's next trip around the sun. Having done this, he was then

19

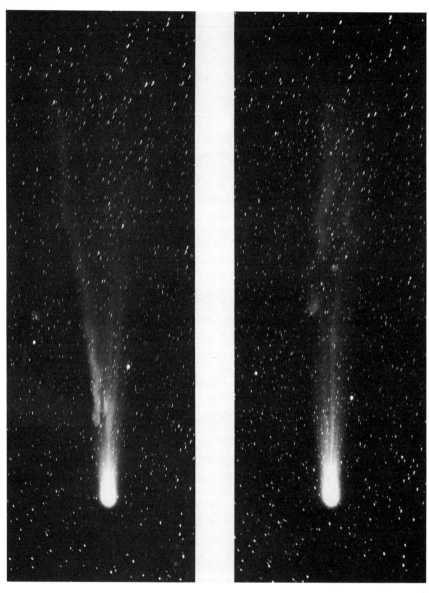

*Two views of Halley's Comet from the Lick Observatory in California on June 6 and 7, 1910.*

able to predict that the comet would be near the earth and sun again on about Christmas of 1758.

Edmund Halley lived to be eighty-six years old, which was an unusually long life for a person born in the 1600s. But he died sixteen years before the date when he thought "his" comet would return. Before he died, he reminded his fellow scientists to watch for the comet. "If it appears," he told them, "please remember it was predicted by an Englishman."

# 3.

# Building on
# the Work of Others

Edmund Halley was not the first person to study comets. He was, however, the one to discover that most comets travel around the sun in elliptical orbits and that each of these comets returns in a certain length of time. This discovery, like all scientific discoveries, was based on the work of many, many other people.

Most people who lived long ago were so afraid of comets that they could not study them carefully. A few of the early scientists, however, believed that comets were not supernatural happenings. One of these was a Roman named Seneca who lived nearly 2,000 years ago. Many people of his day believed that comets were the souls of famous men on their way to Heaven. Other Romans thought that comets caused great disasters. Even the most educated men believed that comets were closer to the earth than the moon was. But Seneca wrote that comets were very much like the planets, in spite of the fact that they looked so different. He also guessed that comets and planets traveled in the same kinds of paths. But he had no proof of these ideas, and they were quickly forgotten.

Many early Chinese scientists also studied comets. For some reason, they never accepted the idea that comets always foretold disaster. Their reports, as we will see, have been very helpful to modern scientists.

Careful study of comets did not begin in Europe until the middle of the sixteenth century. By this time most educated people accepted the idea that the earth and other planets traveled around the sun. Credit for this goes to Nicolaus Copernicus. Copernicus published a book in 1543 in which he described his ideas about how the earth and other planets move around the sun. Before that, people believed that the earth was at the center of the solar system. They thought that the sun, moon, planets, and stars traveled around the earth. As you can see, Copernicus caused a big change in what people believed. The earth went from being at the center of things to being just one of the planets orbiting the sun.

After watching a comet in 1577, an astronomer named Tycho Brahe wrote the first European study of them. He said that comets came from space beyond the farthest planet then known. He also discovered that when a comet was closest to the earth, it was still much, much farther away than the moon.

Tycho Brahe had a student named Kepler. This man also became very interested in comets. He tried to measure the paths of comets in 1607 and in 1618. Johannes Kepler decided that comets traveled through the solar system in nearly straight lines until they got close to the sun. After passing the sun, he said, they then traveled back into space and were lost forever. He guessed that there are as many comets ". . . as there are fishes in the sea."

Kepler also studied the movements of the planets as they

*Nicolaus Copernicus, who suggested that the earth and other planets revolve around the sun, has been honored on many postage stamps.*

traveled around the sun. These studies were very important later to Edmund Halley. Kepler was the first person to realize that planets traveled around the sun in paths that were ellipses rather than in circles. He also discovered that a planet moves faster as it swings around the sun than it does when it is farther away from the sun. Kepler had no idea why this was true.

Often the invention of an instrument makes possible new advances in science. Once scientists had the microscope, they discovered hundreds of different kinds of microorganisms. The rocket and other inventions made possible the astronauts' trips to the moon. And so it was with the invention of the telescope. It is believed that the first telescope was built by Hans Lippershey in 1608. Galileo, a famous Italian scientist, built his first instrument in 1609. With it he discovered sunspots, four moons of Jupiter, and many other things. Once these discoveries were made

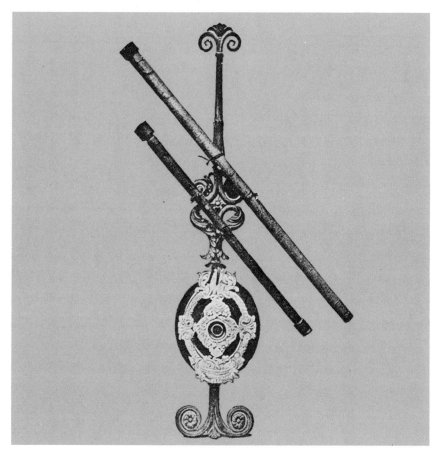

*Galileo's early telescopes are on display in a museum in Florence, Italy.*

known, the telescope quickly became the astronomer's most important tool.

Sir Issac Newton was an English scientist and mathematician. He was interested in the study of gravity. Perhaps you have heard the story about an apple falling from a tree and hitting Newton on the head. This story is probably not true, but some people believe that this is what started Newton on his famous search for an answer to the question of why things fall.

*Famous scientists on postage stamps include Galileo, Kepler, Newton, and Brahe.*

Newton's study of falling objects led to three famous "laws" of science. We now know that these laws do not work well at great distances from the earth. But Newton's Laws of Gravity have helped scientists solve many problems here on earth and also were much used by astronomers in Newton's time.

Newton suggested that the sun and every other object in the sky has gravity. In 1677, he used this mathematical theory to study the paths of the planets. He could explain very nicely how the sun's gravity caused the planets to travel around the sun in elliptical paths rather than in circles. He also could explain why they moved faster the closer they were to the sun. He also suggested that, perhaps, comets might travel in the same type of elliptical paths.

The publication of these ideas was all Edmund Halley needed. Using them, he began his study that led him to predict the return of the comet that today bears his name.

# 4.

# Nature Proves
# Halley Correct

Edmund Halley died in 1742. But his prediction about the return of the comet was not forgotten. Scientists knew that the best way to find out whether or not a theory is correct is to try to use it to predict something that will happen in the future. If the comet did return at Christmas, 1758, it would be strong evidence that Halley was right.

Over and over, teams of astronomers went over Halley's figures. The problem of how to adjust for the effect of the planets on the comet was a difficult one to solve. To predict accurately the pull of gravity between two bodies, you have to know exactly how much each weighs and exactly how far apart they are. Halley had made estimates on both the weights and distances of all the planets known at the time he made his prediction. Based on these estimates, he predicted that the comet would be delayed by the gravity of the planets but would reach the sun by Christmas of 1758. A famous French astronomer named Clairaut said that his figures showed that the gravity of the planets would delay the comet until April, 1759.

All through the fall of 1758, telescopes everywhere in Europe were busy searching that part of the sky in which Halley had told them they would see the comet. It was said that the astronomers of France did not go to bed any night during the entire year, for fear they would miss the comet. But in November of 1758 the comet had not been sighted.

Many people other than scientists also studied the sky. One of these was a German named Johann Georg Palitzsch. He loved to study the stars and the planets in the sky above his farm. To help him in his hobby, he had built a telescope. It was a crude instrument, only 7-feet long. But through it, Palitzsch was the first person to see the return of the comet Edmund Halley had studied. Palitzsch saw it as a fuzzy spot of light on Christmas night, 1758.

This was the date that Halley had predicted the comet would pass closest to the sun. It took the comet nearly three months more to reach the sun. But the figures of astronomers like Clairaut proved that Halley's prediction would have been correct if he had known more about the effect of the gravity of the planets on the comet.

However, Edmund Halley's prediction of the time the comet would reach the sun was off by only three months. Even Clairaut's prediction missed by a month, since the comet reached the sun on March 12, 1759. One reason for these errors was that neither scientist knew that two more huge planets, Uranus and Neptune, were beyond Saturn. These planets were not discovered until 1781 and 1846.

Halley had taken Newton's theories about the orbits of planets and used them to explain the paths of comets. To do this, he had to know a great deal about the figure we call an ellipse.

As noted earlier, an ellipse is like a flattened circle. A circle, as you probably know, is a line around a single center. Circles are easy to draw. Take a piece of paper and tack it to a board. Put a small nail near the center of the paper. Make a loop of string by tying the two ends together. Put one end of the loop of string over the nail in the center of the paper. Put a pencil in the other end of the loop. Hold the string tight as you move the point of the pencil on the paper. With a little practice you will be able to draw a perfect circle.

An ellipse is almost as easy to draw. Put a second nail in the paper a few inches away from the first one. Loop the string around

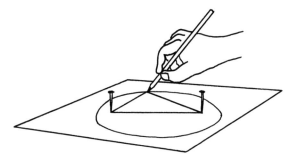

*An ellipse can be drawn using a loop of string, two nails, and a pencil.*

*both* nails. Now, when you move the pencil around at the end of the loop, you will draw an ellipse. The shape of the ellipse will depend on how long the string is and how far apart the nails are. Experiment drawing ellipses by changing the distance between the nails and the length of the loop of string.

The ellipse you draw shows you one possible path of a comet. The sun would be at the place occupied by one of the two nails. The second point (the other nail) would be far out in space.

*Halley's Comet photographed on June 6, 1910, from Beirut (left), Honolulu (center), and Yerkes Observatory in Wisconsin (right).*

Edmund Halley's main theory—that comets travel in elliptical paths around the sun—had been proved by the return of his comet when he predicted its reappearance. To honor the great scientist, the comet was named after him. Every 76 years or so, Halley's Comet fills the night sky. But we are no longer afraid that the strange sight will bring war, disease, or famine. Thanks to Edmund Halley and many other scientists, we know that the great comet is just another of the many wonders of nature.

We have seen how Edmund Halley built his ideas on the work of others, such as Kepler and Newton. As a result of what Halley learned about comets, more and more astronomers turned their attention to the study of the "hairy swords in the sky." Two famous astronomers of the late 1700s and early 1800s were the brother-and-sister team of William and Caroline Herschel. With the aid of larger and larger telescopes they made many important

*Caroline Herschel (right), who discovered at least five comets, and one of the telescopes—this one 40-feet long—used by Caroline and William Herschel.*

discoveries. William discovered the planet Uranus and two of its moons. But it was Caroline who was to discover at least five comets. She was the first woman to discover a comet and became one of the most famous women astronomers of all times.

# 5.

# Halley's Comet and Events in History

Halley had proven that his comet returned to the sun once about every 76 years. He had guessed that the comet of 1682 was the same one that had passed around the sun in 1607 and in 1531. Astronomers were now certain that the comet of 1758–59 was also Halley's Comet.

If the comet had made four trips to the sun, the scientists suspected that it probably had been seen many times before. They began searching the history books and ancient records, looking for mentions of comets that might have been Halley's Comet. This was not an easy job, for two reasons. First, as we have seen, Halley's Comet does not return to the sun *exactly* on a 76-year schedule. The second problem is that ancient records often are hard to find. And these records are sometimes not very accurate.

The scientists subtracted 76 years from the oldest date Halley had found—1531. This gave them an approximate date of 1455. This was the time of a great war between the followers of the Moslem religion and the Christians. The army of the Turks had

*Many peasants in Mexico were so frightened by Halley's Comet in 1910 that they traveled to a shrine to pray for their safety.*

captured Constantinople in 1453. They were also in control of Egypt. In the summer of 1456 the Turkish army attacked the city of Belgrade.

A bright comet lit the sky over the Battle of Belgrade. The Europeans were terribly afraid of comets. They felt that the appearance of a comet foretold disease, death, and disaster. Prayers were said which included the plea that God protect them ". . . from the Devil, the Turks, and the Comet." They were sure that the comet was a sign that the Turks would conquer all of Europe. The Turks did capture Belgrade, but were later defeated and Europe was saved.

Scientists studied the descriptions of the comet's position in the sky in 1456, and its path. They felt certain that this comet over Belgrade was Halley's Comet. Then they looked even further back into the records.

Historical records in Europe before about 1400 are not very complete. And Europeans of that time were so afraid and superstitious about comets that their reports of them are not very accurate. Some modern scientists feel that the early Europeans were so sure that comets brought terrible disasters that they may have written about comets that were never actually seen. They did this as a way of explaining why a war started or why a disease swept through a country.

Even in more modern times, many people have felt this way. Halley's comet was believed to have caused so many terrible disasters that it was called "the bloodiest of all comets" as recently as 1910.

But the early Chinese scientists did not have the same feelings about comets. They observed them carefully. They measured each comet's position and its path across the sky, and they wrote down what they saw. Because of these carefully written records, we are able to trace Halley's Comet and many other comets back more than 2,000 years—to the year 240 B.C. There is even one mention of a comet in 467 B.C. that may have been Halley's Comet.

The Chinese watched a comet for seven weeks in the year A.D. 66. The Old Testament may be describing this comet when it says, "And David lifted up his eyes, and saw the angel of the Lord between the earth and the heaven, having a drawn sword in his hand stretched out over Jerusalem." The city of Jerusalem was then under attack by Roman soldiers. During the siege, disease and famine killed many people. Soon the Romans took the city. We cannot be sure of what the ancient Jews saw just before the fall of the Holy City. But the Chinese records seem to prove that Halley's Comet was making one of its swings around the sun at that time.

In March and April of A.D. 141, the Chinese again reported seeing what must have been Halley's Comet. Soon after the comet disappeared, a terrible disease, the plague, broke out in China and spread throughout the civilized world. In Italy alone an estimated 400,000 people died. Halley's Comet was given the blame by most Europeans, even though the disease did not reach Europe until long after the comet had passed.

In A.D. 451, a spectacular comet was observed in China for thirteen weeks. People in Europe believed this comet was the cause of the Battle of Chalons when the Huns under Attila were defeated by the Roman general, Aetius. It has been estimated that nearly 150,000 soldiers were killed in this battle.

The Chinese astronomers watched and recorded so many comets that sometimes it is difficult to identify Halley's Comet from the rest. However, we are fairly certain that their records describe the return of Halley's Comet in the years 530, 607, 684,

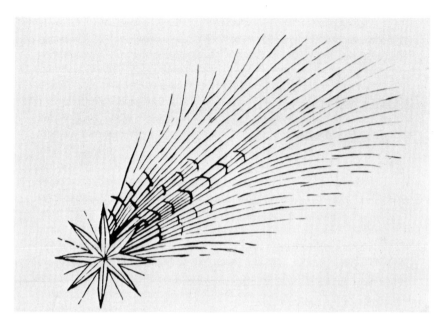

*The oldest known drawing of a comet—Halley's Comet of* A.D. *684—was published in the* Nuremberg Chronicle.

and 760. During each of these years, historians can find terrible disasters to blame on the comet. In 530, the plague swept through Europe. In 607, Slavic peoples were overrunning a good part of Europe. The plague was again widespread in 684; this time the dreadful disease invaded China. Even the terribly cold winter of A.D. 760–61 was thought to have been caused by the comet, which had appeared in the spring before.

The year 1066 is a famous one in English history. This is the year that the Normans, led by William the Conqueror, invaded England. Halley's Comet appeared in the sky every night as the war raged. William took the comet as a sign that his war against the Saxons would succeed. He called the comet "a wonderful sign from Heaven," and used this "sign" to keep his soldiers moving

*William the Conqueror invading England in 1066, with Halley's Comet overhead.*

forward into battle. Later, with the comet fading from sight, William and his Norman army defeated the Saxons at the Battle of Hastings, and conquered England at last.

This historic battle and Halley's Comet are shown on the

famous Bayeux Tapestry. This tapestry is a piece of needlework some 20 inches high and 230 feet long. Red, green, blue, and yellow wool was embroidered into the linen canvas to form the people and inscriptions. The tapestry still is in good condition and is on display in a museum in France.

The terrible Mongol leader, Genghis Khan, thought that comets were his "special stars." Under the 1222 passage of Halley's Comet, his armies slaughtered more than a million people who lived in and around the city of Herat.

At every reappearance of Halley's Comet, one can find a disaster of some kind to associate with it. This is probably true of other comets, too, since for so many years people were truly afraid of the strange light that would appear in the sky. They were ready to blame anything that happened on comets.

*A portion of the famous Bayeux Tapestry shows people watching Halley's Comet.*

# 6.

# Halley's Comet
# in 1835 and 1910

By the early years of the nineteenth century, astronomers were certain that they could accurately predict the return of Halley's Comet. As the time drew near for another visit, they took out their pens and paper and began to work out their predictions. The planet Uranus had been discovered far out beyond Saturn. This gave the scientists more information to work with, since the pull of gravity of the huge planet must affect the path and speed of the comet. Four men published their predictions. All four agreed that Halley's Comet would pass around the sun between November 4 and November 26 in 1835.

For a year before these dates, telescopes swept every inch of sky in the direction from which they expected the comet to appear. Night after night, week after week, the astronomers searched. Finally, on August 6, an Italian scientist found what they had all been looking for. Even though he used one of the world's largest telescopes, the comet was only a faint, misty object. But it was the comet.

*A drawing of Halley's Comet in 1835.*

By September 23, Halley's Comet could be seen without a telescope. And, two days later, people who knew what to look for thought they could see the beginnings of the comet's tail.

Again the superstitious people of the world saw the comet as a sign of disaster. Egypt was struck by a plague called the "Black Death." As many as 9,000 people died in a single night as Halley's Comet appeared late in September of 1835.

By mid-November, everyone in the northern half of the world could see the comet. The tail now stretched across one-sixth of the sky. A huge fire swept New York City as the comet became visible in North America. More than 500 homes burned, along with many office buildings. Was the comet at fault? Many thought so.

Even an Indian uprising is said to have been caused by this visit of Halley's Comet. The Chief of the Seminole Indians in Florida took the "big knife in the sky" as a signal for a war against

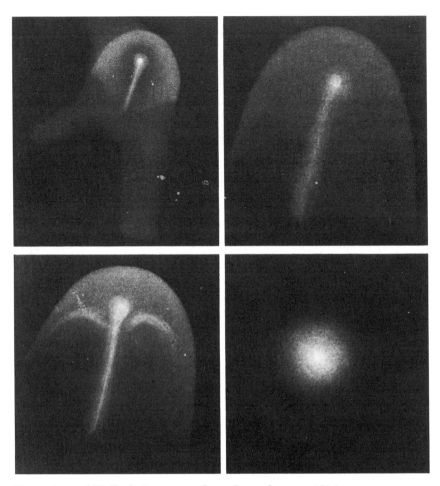

*Four views of Halley's Comet made early in the year 1836.*

the whites at Fort King. All the soldiers in the fort were killed in the attack. Also at this time, the Americans in Texas declared themselves independent of Mexico. The war that followed, including the famous battle at the Alamo, was fought largely during the months that Halley's Comet was passing around the sun. Throughout South America and southern Africa, wars and battles were fought. Each of these was blamed, by some people, on the presence of "the bloodiest comet of them all."

Halley's Comet passed closest to the sun on November 16, 1835. This was within the dates predicted by the scientists several years before. No sooner had the comet passed than they began predicting the comet's next return. The first prediction was for May 24, 1910. Later, the discovery of the planet Neptune caused this date to be changed to April 15, 1910.

This time the watch for Halley's Comet began in late 1908. Now astronomers had larger and better telescopes to work with.

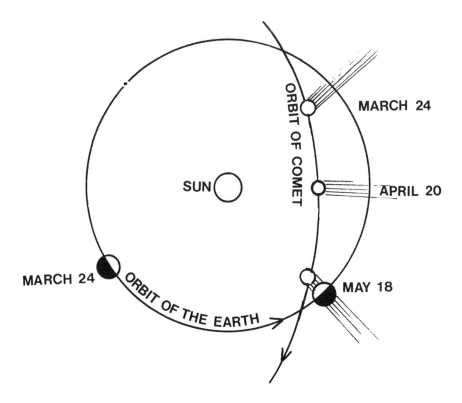

*The passage of Halley's Comet around the sun in 1910.*

They also had another important tool—photography. Instead of just looking through their telescopes, they could now take photographs of the sky through telescopes. Pictures could be taken and then compared with photographs of the same section of the sky taken earlier.

On September 12, 1909, a German astronomer noticed a faint point of light on a photograph he had taken the night before. This small spot did not appear on earlier photographs. Halley's

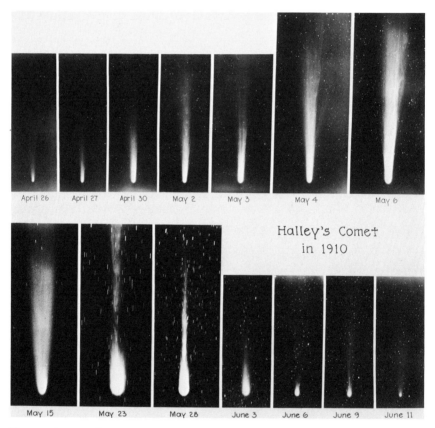

*Views of Halley's Comet made between April 26 and June 11, 1910.*

*A drawing of the tail of Halley's Comet made on May 18, 1910.*

Comet was still 331 million miles from the earth, but it was on its way back to the sun!

The comet gradually got brighter and brighter. It swung around the sun on April 19, only four days later than the scientists had predicted it would.

Within two days Mark Twain died. He was one of America's most famous authors. Perhaps you have read *Tom Sawyer* or *Huckleberry Finn*. It is interesting that Mark Twain died while Halley's Comet was passing around the sun in 1910, because he was born on November 30, 1835. This was just a few days after Halley's Comet had passed on its last visit. "I came in with Halley's Comet," Mark Twain liked to say, "and I'll go out with it."

As the comet reappeared from behind the sun at the end of April, nearly everyone in the world saw a spectacular sight. The Comet's tail reached across nearly one-third of the sky. South of the equator, it was the brightest object in the night sky.

On May 18, Halley's Comet passed between the earth and the sun. The edge of the tail brushed across the earth. Scientists

*This photograph of Halley's Comet taken on June 6, 1910, shows part of the tail drifting away.*

had never been able to see this happen before, so they watched to note what effect it would have on the atmosphere. But a bright, full moon filled the sky with light, and nothing unusual was observed.

The scientists who had predicted that the earth would pass through the tail of the comet believed that a comet's tail was made of very thin gas. Therefore, they did not expect anything very

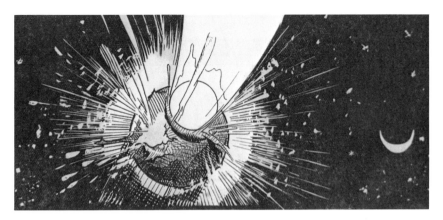

*An artist's conception of what would happen if Halley's Comet crashed into the earth.*

exciting to happen. But their prediction caused a great deal of panic among people who did not know much about science. One group of people in Asia thought, for some strange reason, that they would be killed unless they got into water up to their necks. Water barrels were filled to the top. The people waited for the terrible event, ready to jump into the barrels at the approach of the comet's tail.

All over the world, people were sure the end was near. Some were certain that the tail of the comet was made of poisonous gases that would kill everyone on earth. Other people feared that the head of the comet would brush close to the earth and throw the earth out of its path around the sun. Still others were afraid the comet would smash directly into the earth and destroy it. One writer suggested that the "fiery torch" of the comet would set fire to the hydrogen gas in the earth's atmosphere. This, he predicted, would leave the entire world ". . . a seething ocean of flame."

These people must have been very relieved when nothing happened.

# 7.

# The Second Return in the 20th Century

$A$s time grew near for the second return of Halley's Comet in the twentieth century, astronomers again began to try to figure out the exact date of its swing around the sun. But now, for the first time, they did not have to use pen and paper and take thousands of hours to get their answers. Instead, they fed their information into high-speed computers. Within minutes, the answers came back. Halley's Comet would swing around the sun on February 9, 1986.

The computers gave the modern scientists much more information than this about the famous comet. It told them exactly where to point their telescopes in order to take the first photographs of the comet, and when—toward the end of 1984. The computer also told them the dates that the comet might be most easily seen without a telescope—in mid-November of 1985 in the northern hemisphere and around April 15, 1986, south of the equator.

Using the computer and the records of past visits by the

comet, one astronomer made another interesting prediction. He had carefully studied the pull of gravity of all nine planets on the comet. He also tried to determine the exact dates the comet has gone around the sun in the past. This scientist felt that the pull of gravity of the nine planets is not enough to explain why the comet's orbit takes more time on some trips than on others. His figures led him to believe that there is a tenth planet out beyond Pluto. He predicted that astronomers will eventually find a planet three times the size of Saturn, going around the sun once in approximately 500 years. So far, no one has been able to find such a planet, but the search goes on.

One thing the computers could not predict for the scientists was the amount of pollution in the earth's atmosphere in 1985–86. Scientists had predicted that everyone would be able to see a new comet in 1974. This comet was named Comet Kohoutek, after its discoverer. Everyone was very excited about being able to see it. But the haze of pollution that hung over American cities in 1974, plus the light given off by our buildings and streetlights, made it impossible for most people to see the comet. Many miles away from the cities, in the darker, cleaner air of the rural areas, people had a chance to see the comet more clearly.

The scientists knew that outdoor lighting in the United States had increased by 1970 to ten times what it had been in 1960. By 1985, they feared, the only people who would be able to see Halley's Comet would be those who lived in the most rural areas, and those who were willing to travel far away from the cities.

As early as 1972, scientists were beginning to describe the second return of Halley's Comet in the twentieth century in great detail. By the end of October or early November of 1985, they said, the comet would be seen in the eastern sky just before dawn.

49

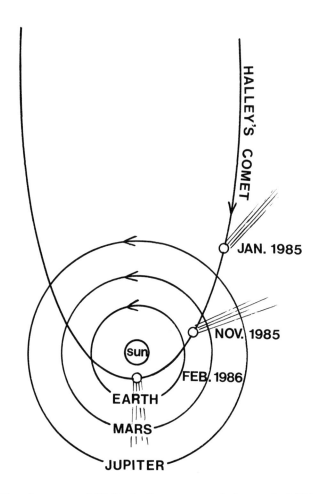

*The predicted passage of Halley's Comet around the sun in 1986.*

At this time, it probably would not have much of a tail. But by the end of December, they predicted, those people who were willing to look for it carefully should be able to see a fairly long tail. Mid-January of 1986 should find the comet quite a bit brighter and in the western sky at dusk.

The best view of Halley's Comet on this trip will be south of the equator. After it passes around the sun between January 25 and February 20, it would be well south of the equator. But, astronomers predicted, those of us living in the United States might still see it low in the southeast just before dawn. In April, they figured, the comet would be seen in the west late in the evening.

The United States space agency (NASA) and the space agencies of other countries have considered many plans for sending instruments as close to the comet as they could. Some of these plans were fantastic experiments. Most were too expensive to be taken seriously. But the ideas are interesting.

The scientists at NASA came up with a plan for pushing the instruments to the comet. They wanted to use the same force that

*An artist's conception of the solar sail designed to carry instruments out to Halley's Comet and study it close-by.*

pushes the comet's tail away from the head—the light from the sun. They wanted the instruments to sail through space pushed by the "solar wind."

They suggested that they could build a huge square sail, nearly half a mile on each side. The sail would be made of very, very thin and shiny plastic. It would be painted black on the side away from the sun.

The collapsed sail and the 11,000 pounds of instruments needed to study the comet could be carried out into space on a space shuttle. Once in orbit around the earth, the sail could be attached to the instruments and the whole thing pushed out away from the earth. The force of the light against the shiny side of the sail would, they hoped, push the "ship" to speeds of nearly 200,000 miles an hour. With this device, the scientists thought they might get their cameras and other instruments to within a mile of the comet's head.

# 8.

# What Is a Comet?

When Edmund Halley accurately predicted the return of his comet, he proved that it moved in an elliptical path. Since Halley's time, many scientists have studied the paths of thousands of comets. They have found that the time it takes one comet to make a round trip may be very different from the time it takes another comet. Some comets make their trip around the sun in less time than it takes the outer planets to make one orbit. Pluto, the farthest planet away from the sun that we know about, takes nearly 250 years to go around the sun one time. Neptune, the next planet in toward the sun, makes one orbit every 165 years.

Comets that return to the sun at least once every 200 years are often called "short-period comets." The paths of these comets do not carry them very far beyond the edge of our solar system. Halley's Comet is a good example of a short-period comet.

About 40 comets have orbits that carry them only as far away as the orbit of the huge planet, Jupiter. These comets make an

*Comet Kohoutek photographed on January 15, 1974. Its orbit is so large that it will not return to the sun for over 70,000 years.*

orbit around the sun in less than twelve years. Some of them make the trip in less than four years. Many scientists think that these comets probably had larger orbits at one time, but were caught by the strong pull of Jupiter's gravity and thrown into a much shorter orbit.

"Long-period comets" take more than 200 years to orbit the the sun. Many take hundreds and even thousands of years to make one trip around the sun and back again.

Over 500 comets have been discovered that have orbits that are so large there is no historical evidence that the comet has ever visited the sun before. Scientists think that some of these comets have orbits that carry them out into deep space, rather than in an elliptical orbit around the sun.

All of our planets go around the sun in the same direction. About half of the known comets, however, go around the sun in the opposite direction. No one understands why this is so. But it is interesting that all but three of the known short-period comets go in the same direction around the sun as the planets do. Two of these "backward comets" take more than 150 years to make their complete trip around the sun. Some scientists think that these comets might not really be short-period comets. The only "backward comet" that is definitely a short-period comet is our old friend, Halley's Comet.

While scientists feel that they understand the type of paths followed by comets fairly well, they do not agree on what comets are made of. The closest to the earth a comet has ever come, in modern times, is about $3\frac{1}{2}$ million miles. The best astronomers have been able to do is look at comets through their telescopes and study them with other instruments from a great distance.

If you were to look at a comet without a telescope you would see two parts—the head, or *coma*, and the tail. Through powerful telescopes, some comets also seem to have a starlike object inside the head. Scientists call this object the *nucleus*, but are not sure what it is. Some believe that the nucleus is not anything special, but just part of the coma.

Because some scientists believe the coma contains a nucleus and others do not, there are two theories used to explain what comets are. It may be that there are really two kinds of comets, or it may be that neither of these theories is correct.

According to the "dirty snowball" theory, when the comet is far away from the sun, it is a ball of frozen gases. This ball is also thought to contain millions of small dust particles.

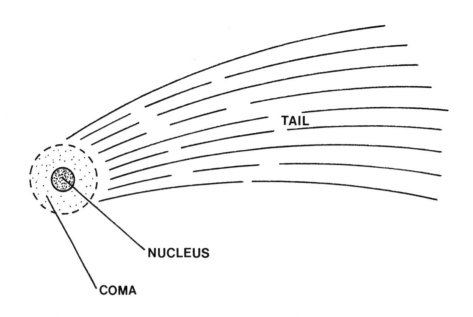

TAIL

NUCLEUS

COMA

*A comet is believed to be made up of the coma, the nucleus, and the tail.*

As the "dirty snowball" gets closer to the sun, its outer layers become warmer. As this happens, it begins to melt back into gases. These gases glow in the light of the sun, much like a fluorescent light glows when electrical energy affects the gas inside the tube. According to this theory, the nucleus of a comet is made up of the unmelted center and solid bits of dust of the "dirty snowball."

The second theory calls a comet a "flying sandbank." This theory says that perhaps the coma of the comet is a huge cloud made up mainly of dust particles. The nucleus that is thought to be seen in the heads of some comets is explained with the idea that the dust particles are closer together near the center of the coma. This would, some scientists think, make the head look like it has a more solid center. The dust particles of the "flying sandbank" would glow from the light of the sun as they got closer to it.

The tail of a comet is the most spectacular part. In some comets, the tail seems to reach nearly from horizon to horizon.

Not all comets have huge tails, though. In some comets, the tail is very short and looks like a bulge on the coma. Other comets have no tail at all, especially if they are seen when they are a long way from the sun.

The tail of a comet always points away from the sun. This fact was discovered by early Chinese astronomers. A comet in the western sky at evening and a comet in the eastern sky at dawn will both have tails that seem to point upward.

When a comet is first seen, far out in space, it will usually not have a tail. As the comet gets closer and closer to the sun, the tail seems to grow. Then, after the comet swings around the sun and heads back into space, its tail gets shorter and shorter.

Early astronomers could not explain why comets grew tails as they approached the sun. Newton suggested that some kind of force from the sun pushed part of the comet's head out away from the sun. Modern scientists think that Newton may have made a pretty good guess.

We are now fairly certain that there are at least two types of comet tails. One type is made up of gases from the coma. This kind of comet tail is pushed out away from the coma by streams of sub-atomic particles from the sun. This has been called "solar wind." The second type of comet's tail is made up of solid dust particles. These tiny bits of solid material are pushed away from the coma by the pressure of the light from the sun. When a comet's tail is made up only of gases, it will usually seem to be very straight and very narrow. A tail made up of mostly solid dust particles will generally be wider and more curved.

Even the dust-particle tails of comets are made up of a very small amount of material. When the earth passed through the

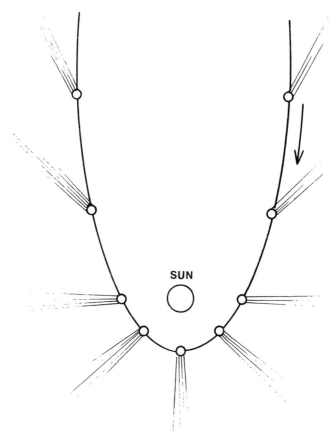

*The tail of a comet always points away from the sun.*

tail of Halley's Comet in 1910, it ran into so few bits of material that no one on earth noticed any effects.

It will be difficult for astronomers to learn much more about comets from the surface of the earth. The earth is surrounded by a thick layer of air called the atmosphere. This air in the atmosphere keeps many of our scientific tools from making any better observations of comets than those that already have been made.

In 1968, NASA launched a set of instruments into orbit

around the earth. These telescopes, cameras, and other instruments allowed astronomers to study space without having to look first through the atmosphere.

In 1970, these instruments were turned toward two comets. An unexpected discovery was made. Both comets were found to be surrounded by huge clouds of the gas hydrogen. Around one, the Comet Bennett, the scientists found a cloud of gas eight times larger than our sun! This discovery excited astronomers everywhere. But more observations like these will be needed before we can be sure about what comets are made of.

# 9.

# Tips for Comet Watchers

**D**o you remember what Kepler said about the number of comets in our solar system? He felt that they were as numerous as the "fishes in the sea." Modern scientists agree that there are a huge number of comets. No one knows how many, of course. Some scientists suspect that there are hundreds or thousands, while others say there must be millions of comets.

Unfortunately, many, many of these comets are so far away as they swing around the sun that we cannot see them. Other comets are closer, but too small to be seen from earth.

Every year, however, a dozen or more comets come within reach of the telescopes and binoculars of the comet watchers on earth. Two or three of these yearly visitors are comets that have never been identified before. Most of them are old friends, like Halley's Comet, that visit the sun on a regular schedule.

These periodic comets—the ones that return time after

time—have been carefully studied. A group of amateur comet watchers who are members of the British Astronomical Association have listed all of these comets in a catalog. This book gives the orbits of each of the periodic comets. The information tells the comet watcher where to look for comets and when. It can also be used to identify the comet by name. If a comet is spotted that is not in the right place and following the right orbit, it is considered to be a new comet.

When comets are first sighted, they are given labels such as 1983a and 1983b. The first comet sighted in 1983 is 1983a, the second one is labeled 1983b, and so on. Later, they are put in order of the dates each comet actually passed closest to the sun. This order is shown by roman numerals. So, they become 1983 I, 1983 II, 1983 III, and so forth. If the comets are new ones, they will also be given the names of their discoverers. Since comets are often seen by more than one person at about the same time, some comets may have as many as three names. For example, the seventh comet to pass around the sun in 1967 was a new one. It was reported by three comet hunters. So, its official name is Mitchell-Jones-Gerber (1967 VII).

At least three careful measurements of the position of a new comet are needed in order to figure out what its orbit is, and therefore be certain it is a new comet. No two comets look exactly the same. Even periodic comets, those that return time after time, do not always look the same. The size of the tail changes, of course, as the comet gets closer to the sun. Sometimes the tail is split into two or more parts. And the brightness of the comet's coma changes from night to night.

Some comets can be seen for only a few days. Others will seem to hang in the sky without moving very much for many

*Halley's Comet on May 3, 1910, showing a split in the end of the tail.*

months. The Comet Stearns (1927 IV) was watched through large telescopes for nearly four years.

Sometimes comets do not return to earth on schedule. They are seen once, and their orbits show that they should be periodic comets, but they do not return. Sometimes the comet will return several times, right on schedule, and then disappear forever.

One example of these lost comets was Lexell's Comet. It was first discovered in 1770 on the first day of July of that year. The spectacular comet was said to be five times brighter than the full moon. Its discoverer figured that his comet would return in less than six years. But it did not. And it has never been seen again.

Astronomers think they have finally solved the mystery of the sudden appearance and disappearance of the comet. The orbit Lexell figured for his comet showed that as it moved toward the sun it passed very close to the planet Jupiter. The strong pull of gravity of the planet must have pulled the comet into a new orbit that brought it very close to the earth. Then, as the comet left the sun, it again passed close to Jupiter. This time, the pull of the planet threw the comet into a new orbit that carried it so far away from the earth that we cannot see it.

Scientists believe that some comets may have been broken into smaller comets by passing too close to a planet or to the sun. If this is true, it may explain some of the lost comets. It may help us understand an interesting group of comets called "sungrazers."

Sungrazers are groups of small comets. Their orbits are very much alike. All of them pass so close to the sun that they seem to "graze" its surface.

Because they are so close to the sun, the sungrazers are often very, very bright. Many can be seen during the daytime, and some have spectacular tails. A few have been seen to split into several parts as they neared the sun. Unfortunately for many of us, sungrazers are more often seen from the southern half of the earth than from locations north of the equator.

Some comets can be seen without the use of telescopes or binoculars. But the use of even low-powered instruments will allow you to observe many comets that cannot be seen without them. Binoculars that only magnify objects six or seven times will be of great help to the amateur comet watcher.

# 10.

# Comet Hunting

Comet hunting is quite different from comet watching. The comet hunter searches the sky in hopes of finding a new, unnamed comet. The successful hunter may have the honor of having a comet named after him or her.

It is not necessary to be a professional scientist, working with a huge telescope and camera, in order to be a comet hunter. Indeed, these instruments are rarely used to search for comets. When they are used in the study of comets, they are generally turned toward the very faint comets—those that are far away from the sun. Thus, they are most often busy searching the skies at midnight, when the sun is on the opposite side of the earth. This leaves a large part of the night sky for the amateur comet hunter to search in.

Comets are brightest when they are closest to the sun. Therefore, you may find your comet in the western sky just after sunset, or in the east just before dawn. A small telescope or a good pair of binoculars, a good star map and a catalog of comets, a good

*Binoculars, a flashlight, and a star finder are useful tools in comet watching and comet hunting.*

view of the horizon, and a lot of patience are the only tools you will need. In many cases, a comfortable lawn chair also comes in handy.

The instruments you use are very important. Some telescopes and binoculars give you a wide-angle view of the sky. These may be called "rich field" instruments. They are great for comet watching, studying the moon, the planets, or even the larger galaxies. But they take in too much light to be of much use to the comet hunter. The low power of these "rich field" instruments also makes it difficult to see a very dim comet.

Most comet hunters prefer to use binoculars rather than telescopes. Binoculars are easier to carry and store than are

*Many comet watchers use a small telescope.*

*A reclining lawn chair makes comet watching more enjoyable.*

telescopes. They are also easier to use because you can leave both eyes open. Many comet hunters like to use war-surplus binoculars of the 20 x 100 or 25 x 105 size. The first number (20 and 25) tells how many times the binoculars magnify the object you are looking at. The second (100 and 105) is the distance in millimeters across the front lenses.

A word of caution: When using telescopes and binoculars,

*never* point them toward the sun or a bright light while you are looking through them. These instruments can focus the sun's rays into a strong beam of light that can cause eye damage or even blindness. Perhaps you have seen how a small magnifying glass can be used to start a fire!

Comet hunting can take a lot of time. Mark Whitaker, a sixteen-year-old student, found his first comet in 1968 after only three nights of searching. But this is very unusual. Most hunters search the sky carefully, night after night, for years without finding a new comet. But this is why amateur astronomers have such a good chance of making a new discovery. Finding new comets takes a great deal of time, and professional scientists cannot afford to spend their time looking for them. Chances are, the next new comet to be discovered will be found by an amateur comet hunter, and it can be you.

The first thing a comet hunter must do is learn the sky well. You are going to search only a small part of the sky close to either the western or eastern horizon. So you do not have to learn all of the stars at once—just those in your search area.

Even so, you will see many, many more objects through your telescope or binoculars than you will be able to observe with your naked eyes. You will see clusters of stars and even whole galaxies so far away that they look like fuzzy blobs. These are easily mistaken for distant comets. A good star map will identify most of these for you. The others will have to be watched carefully for several hours, or even on two or more different nights, until you are certain they are not moving, and therefore not comets.

You will find that you must let your eyes get used to the dark before you can see well through your telescope or binoculars. This may take an hour or more. Any time you look at something in a bright light, your eyes will have to start all over again getting used

*Many of the photographs of Halley's Comet in this book were taken at Yerkes Observatory in Williams Bay, Wisconsin.*

to the dark. Therefore, when you stop to read your star map, you should use a dim, *red* light. You may wish to try wrapping a piece of red plastic around the end of a flashlight. If there are any streetlights near you, you may want to hide under a blanket or inside a large box and stick only the end of your telescope or binoculars outside. Oftentimes it is possible to get in the shadow of a house or other structure.

You must set up a pattern for carefully searching the part of the sky in which you are interested. The brighter, well-known stars and other objects in the sky will be your signposts. Soon you will begin to recognize them as old friends.

The fainter objects you will see are often fascinating, too. Whole galaxies, millions of light years away, will also soon become familiar neighbors.

Then, one night, there is a faint, fuzzy stranger. You check its position carefully with the familiar objects around it. Over several hours it changes its place in the sky just a little. Once you are fairly certain it is a comet, you should notify the International Astronomical Union in Cambridge, Massachusetts, that you have found your comet.

But be sure of your discovery before you tell the world. You can imagine how embarrassed one well-known astronomer was when he reported the discovery of a new comet and it turned out that he was looking at a blob of snow on a nearby telephone line.

Many new comets are discovered by people who are not hunting for them. In 1910, a group of diamond workers discovered a daylight comet while walking home from work. In 1961, an airline hostess spotted an early morning comet when she glanced out the window of the airplane. A comet was seen in 1947 by a British sailor who was on watch while his ship sailed through the South Atlantic Ocean. All of these people were looking in the right direction at the right time. So, keep your eyes open. Your comet may be in the sky tonight!

# Appearances of Halley's Comet

| * Dates | | Comments |
|---|---|---|
| B.C. | 467 | First mention of a comet in historical records that may have been Halley's Comet |
| | 240 | First definite sighting by Chinese astronomers of comet later to be identified as Halley's Comet |
| | 87 | Appearance described in Chinese records |
| | 11 | Observed by both Chinese and Roman astronomers |
| A.D. | 66 | At time of attack on the city of Jerusalem by the Romans |
| | 141 | At time of a great plague |

* The average length of time between appearances of Halley's Comet is 76 years. However, the comet's period may be as little as 75 years and as much as 79 years. Most of these differences in the comet's period are the results of variations in gravity due to the positions of the planets. Reporting the comet's return to the nearest year also can have an effect. For example, if the comet appears one time in December and the next time in early January, the dates suggest another year when the time really may have been only a few days. Another factor is that observers may have reported the dates in different ways—when the comet first appeared, when it was brightest, when it was closest to the sun, or when it disappeared.

| | |
|---|---|
| 218 | Civil war in China |
| 295 | Observed in China |
| 374 | Observed in China |
| 451 | At time of the Battle of Chalons when Huns were defeated by the Romans |
| 530 | Plague in Europe |
| 607 | Parts of Europe overrun by Slavic peoples |
| 684 | Plague invades China; earliest drawing of Halley's Comet published in the *Nuremberg Chronicle* |
| 760 | Especially cold winter blamed on comet |
| 837 | King Louis of France died shortly after appearance of the comet |
| 912 | Recorded by Japanese observers; war in Europe |
| 989 | Described in European and Chinese records; war in Europe |
| 1066 | William the Conqueror invaded England and defeated the Saxons at the Battle of Hastings |
| 1145 | Pope Eugenius III saw the comet as a call for a Holy war against the Moslems |
| 1222 | Genghis Khan thought the comet was his "special star"; more than a million people were killed by his armies |
| 1301 | War in Europe |

| | |
|---|---|
| 1378 | Observed in China and Europe |
| 1456 | At time of a great war between Christians and Moslems |
| 1531 | Halley suspected that this comet and the one that appeared in 1607 were the same comet he saw in 1682 |
| 1607 | Kepler tried to measure the path of the comet |
| 1682 | The comet observed and studied by Edmund Halley |
| 1758 | Appearance correctly predicted by Halley |
| 1835 | The "Black Death" in Egypt; battle of The Alamo; Mark Twain was born |
| 1910 | Viewed and photographed through improved telescopes; Mark Twain died |
| 1986 | Second appearance of Halley's Comet in the twentieth century |

# Index

Norman D. Anderson lives in Raleigh, North Carolina, where he is a Professor of Science Education at North Carolina State University. Walter R. Brown lives in Virginia Beach, Virginia, where he taught junior high school science for several years.

Both Dr. Anderson and Dr. Brown received their Ph.D.'s in science education at Ohio State University and they have been writing books together since their graduate days. They are the coauthors of a science textbook series that is used in middle and junior high schools throughout the country. They also have co-authored several books in the Historical Catastrophes Series, the most recent titles being *Catastrophes* and *Sea Disasters*.